MW00464020

Python

Machine

Learning

Machine learning: basic concepts + artificial intelligence + Python programming + Python machine learning. A complete guide to building intelligent systems using Python libraries

Table of Contents

Furthermore, the transmission, duplication, or reproduction of any of the following work including specific information will be considered an illegal act irrespective of if it is done electronically or in print. This extends to creating a secondary or tertiary copy of the work or a recorded copy and is only allowed with the express written consent from the Publisher. All additional right reserved.

The information in the following pages is broadly considered a truthful and accurate account of facts and as such, any inattention, use, or misuse of the information in question by the reader will render any resulting actions solely under their purview. There are no scenarios in which the publisher or the original author of this work can be in any fashion deemed liable for any hardship or damages that may befall them after undertaking information described herein.

Additionally, the information in the following pages is intended only for informational purposes and should thus be thought of as universal. As befitting its nature, it is presented without assurance regarding its prolonged validity or interim quality. Trademarks that are mentioned are done without written consent and can in no way be considered an endorsement from the trademark holder.

Introduction

Congratulations on purchasing *Python Machine Learning* and thank you for doing so.

The following chapters will discuss everything that you need to know in order to get started with Python machine learning. Machine learning is a growing field, one that is taking over the world of technology and helping us to do and learn things like never before. And when you add in some of the cool things that you are able to do with the Python language along with it, you will find that this kind of learning is easy to work with as well.

The beginning of this guidebook is going to spend some time looking at machine learning and what it all entails. We will look at the basics of machine learning as well as some of the most common types of machine learning including supervised and unsupervised machine learning. Once we have a good idea of how we can work with machine learning, it is time to move on to a bit of work with Python. We will explore how to set up our Python environment to work with machine learning, before moving on to some different things that you can do with Python machine learning including data pre-proccing, linear regression, and more!

Once we have the ideas of machine learning and Python all setup, it is time to learn a lot of the other things that you will be able to do when it comes to machine learning. We will look at how to work with decision trees and random forests, support vector regressions, Naïve Bayes problems and KNN classification problems. To end this guidebook, we will look at data wrangling visualization, web applications, and accelerated data analysis that can be done with the help of the Python language.

There are so many things that you are able to do when it comes to machine learning, and this is a field that is going to grow and grow over time. Make sure to check out this guidebook to help you get started learning how to work with Python machine learning!

There are plenty of books on this subject on the market, thanks again for choosing this one! Every effort was made to ensure it is full of as much useful information as possible, please enjoy!

Chapter 1: Support Vector Regression Problems

Another topic that you are able to work with when it comes to Python machine learning is SVR or Support Vector Regression. This is going to be one of the types of support vector machine algorithm that you can work with, and it works well whether you are trying to do a linear regression or a non-linear regression. This type of algorithm has been around since the 160s and it is one of the most famous of all the algorithms that you are able to use in machine learning. Before the idea of neural networks is as common and well-used as they are today, SVM was the most accurate algorithm that you were able to use when you wanted to work in machine learning.

In this chapter, we will take a look at this kind of algorithm and the intuition that you are able to find with it. We will also take a look at how this kind of algorithm is going to work. First, though, we have to take a look at the theory that comes with the support vector machine algorithm.

The theory that comes with SVM

When we are looking at the linear regression that is typical or one that is found in a space that is two-dimensional, the job here is to find a straight line that is able to bisect as many of the points of data as is possible in a straight line or a curve. These sounds good in general, but remember that there are times in the real world that there are multiple decision boundaries that can be used to classify the data points. And then, if you decide to add in some data points at some point, then the boundary for the decision that you choose will decide how you will apply and classify these data points.

The whole job that comes with this kind of algorithm is that it is responsible to help you find a decision boundary that works well to classify your data. You want to make sure that the accuracy is as good as possible and that there is a minimal amount of misclassification in the process. The way that the SVM algorithm is able to do this will be able to maximize the distance between the closest data points from all of the classes that are in the set of data.

When you use this kind of algorithm, you will find that these boundaries are discoverable with the help of its support vectors, which is how it is going to get its name in the process. When looking at the charts, the support vectors are the ones that will pass through the closest data points of the two classes you want to work with. The job here is to maximize the distance that occurs between the two vectors.

The next thing that you are going to look for is a line that will run parallel to both of these support vectors. You want to try and draw it right in the middle of the two vectors to get the best results. This is going to be the decision boundary so you want it to be as accurate as possible. And it is going to give you a good idea of how your information is split up so you can make some better decisions in the process.

This kind of algorithm is going to be used any time that you end up having a ton of data that doesn't seem to have one vector line that is going to pass through it very well, so you work with two of them to help you separate out of this data to help you out. You will use these vectors to make sure that you can look at both sets of data, separating it out into two sets and sometimes more. You can then take a look at the categories and found out which one is going to be the best with the information that you need, check out the two groups are the similar, and how both of them are different. You can then separate this information out and then have important business decisions made from this.

Support Vector Regression is going to help you to make some important data decisions. There are times when your information is not going to fit into one group or near one line, and this kind of chart is going to make a big difference in how you separate out the information that you need. This can help you to really explore the data that you have, and it will help you to make some of the comparisons and more for your own business.

MACHINELEARING EPISODE: 1

UNDERSTANDING
PYTHON
ECOSYSTEM

@METADESIGNIDEAS

NUMPY   PANDAS   KERAS
TENSORFLOW   THEANO
SCIKIT-LEARN   MATPLOTLIB

Chapter 2: Naïve Bayes Problems and Python Machine Learning

Now we need to move on to working with the Naïve Bayes machine learning algorithm. We have spent some time so far in this guidebook looking at the different regression algorithms that you are able to work with. For this algorithm, we are going to take a look at some of the classification problems that you are able to work with. And the first of these algorithms that we are going to take a look at is the Naïve Bayes.

Naïve Bayes is going to be a type of supervised machine learning like we talked about ahead of time. And it is going to get its basis in the Bayes Theorem. This algorithm is going to be based on the idea that the independence feature. This states that a feature that is found in a data set doesn't end up having any kind of relationship with one another.

For example, you may find that fruit is going to be a banana if it is five inches long or more, had a diameter that is at least a centimeter, and it is yellow in color. But when you are working with the Naïve Bayes algorithm, you are not going to have any concerns about these features or about how these features are going to depend on each other. The fruit will be declared as a banana with the independent contribution of the various features. This is why it is a Naïve algorithm.

When it comes to working in machine learning, this kind of algorithm is going to be seen as one of the most simple machine learning algorithms, but there is going to be a lot of power that comes with it. And that is why we are going to take a look at it a bit in this chapter.

First, we need to take a look at some of the advantages that you are able to get when it comes to using the Naïve Bayes algorithm. This will help us learn more about this algorithm. There are a lot of different benefits that come with this learning algorithm, and some of the ones you should consider include:

1. The Naïve Bayes algorithm is really simple to work with, and you can train employees on how to use it quickly. It isn't going to have a huge amount of math that goes with it, and you won't have to deal with backpropagation or any error correction to deal with it either. This makes it

easy to use in a lot of different data that you want to look through.

2. You will find that the Naïve Bayes algorithm is one that can perform the best, especially compared to a lot of the other algorithms that you can choose to work with when it comes to categorical data. If you are using this for some numeric features, then this is going to be an algorithm that is going to assume a distribution that is normal.

While many companies find that working with the Naïve Bayes algorithm because it is such a simple one to use and easy to understand, there are a few disadvantages to working with this kind of algorithm, and there are times when it is better to work with something different. It works in many situations and can make things easier for you, but there are times when you will want to use it in a different manner.

To start, when you are working with data from the real world, you will find that the features you use will be mostly dependent on the other kinds of features who are there. the assumption of independence that comes with this algorithm is going to be a bad way to predict any data that has an independent feature that comes with it. You have to take this into consideration when you decide to work with it.

Another negative that can come with this is when you decide to work with some categorical features. This could be a value in a test set that may not be found in your training set. When this happens, then the Naïve Bayes algorithm will then automatically assign a probability of zero to that instance. What this means is that the programmer or whoever handles this is going to need to go through and do some cross-validation over any of the results to make sure it works properly when using this algorithm.

Now that we understand some of the benefits and negatives that come with this algorithm, it is time to take a look at all of the different ways that you are able to use this algorithm. Sure, there are going to be times when you may need to check the results and when you may not get the results that you would like. But it does work well and can provide you with the answers that you need. A few of the different ways that you are going to be able to benefit when you use this kind of algorithm will include:

1. The Naïve Bayes algorithm is often going to be used when it comes to problems that are multi-class and ones that are used for text classification. This may include a few things like spam filtering in emails and any kind of sentimental analysis.

2. This is an algorithm that can be used in many cases to help out with any collaborative filtering algorithms. These are going to be used when the programmer would like to make a

recommendation system that is based on machine learning.

3. Programmers will often find that Naïve Bayes is going to be faster compared to some of the other algorithms out there while giving comparable results. This makes it a lot easier to use this algorithm in some applications that are done in real time.

There are many times when you are going to want to work with the Naïve Bayes algorithm. It has a lot of power behind it, without taking as much time and effort as some of the others. While it only works with some of the classification problems that you want to work with, and it is going to require you to do a little bit of work to check the problems, it is still one of the best-supervised machine learning methods that you are able to use.

Machine Learning with Python Course and E-Book

Chapter 3: K-Nearest Neighbors for Classification Problems

Another type of machine learning algorithm that you are going to enjoy using, based on the data that you want to work with and what you want to get out of the data, is the K-nearest neighbors, or the KNN, algorithm. Many programmers like to work with this kind of method when they have some data from the real world, and this data doesn't seem to follow a trend. While we all wish the data that we had would follow a nice trend, this is just not something that tends to happen all that much. This machine learning algorithm is going to help you to deal with this kind of data.

The main kind of idea that you are going to be able to see with the KNN algorithm is simple. This algorithm is going to work to find the distance between your new points of data and then compare it to the older data points that you already added into it. Then the algorithm will take this a bit further and will rank all of your points of data, going in ascending order based on how far they are from your testing point. The KNN algorithm will be able to take all of this information, and all of the points that you have, and will choose the top K-nearest data points. Then it has the information and assigns new points of data to the class that has the most K data points.

You may get into this kind of algorithm and hear some programmers call this a lazier algorithm, rather than one that is eager. What this means is that with this learning algorithm, it is not going to take a look at any data for training to help it come up with the results. This algorithm is not going to work with a training phase, and if there is one that is added in to be careful and to add in more accuracy, it is small.

There are benefits to this of course. First off, it means that the training phase with this set of data is going to be fast. And since there is a lack of generalization that occurs, it means that the KNN algorithm is able to use all of the data that you add in for training. During the testing phase, you are going to use more of the data points that you have, which increases the accuracy.

Another reason that the KNN algorithm is going to be so important to sort out your data is that it is basing itself on the idea of similarity. This means that it is focused on how closely any of the sample features will be to the training. And the similarity that shows up with the data is going to help you to classify it a bit better.

As you can guess with this one, the KNN algorithm is going to be used when you have a problem that needs classification. Any object or data point that you add into the mix is going to be classified using the majority vote of all the data points that are near it. The end goal that comes with this one is that all of the points should be classified and assigned to a point that is as similar to it as possible. That data point needs to be similar to all of its nearest neighbors as well, otherwise, this doesn't work the way that you want.

You may find as you work with the KNN algorithm that there are certain times where you can bring it up with some regression problems. However, this is not that common and many times it is going to be less accurate than what you see when you use it with the classification problems. For the most part, the KNN algorithm is going to be used in problems of classification.

How am I able to use the KNN algorithm

As you can guess from the discussion we just had, there are a lot of different ways that the KNN algorithm can come into play. Some of the different applications for this algorithm are going to include:

- Credit ratings: Many times the KNN algorithm will be used to help with credit ratings. First, you will collect financial characteristics and then will compare that information with people who have similar financial features in the database. Just by the nature that comes with a credit rating, those who have similar details financially would end up getting the same kind of credit rating. This means that you could take a database that is already in existence and use it to help predict the credit rating of a new customer, without having to go through and perform all the calculations again.

- Many times when a bank is considering giving out a loan to someone, they may use a KNN algorithm. They may want to ask if they should give an individual a loan? Is it likely that an individual is going to default on their loan? Does the person look like they have characteristics of others who have defaulted on their loans, or are they closer to those who haven't defaulted on their loans? The KNN algorithm can help you compare the information you have against information that is in the database and then answer these questions.

- The KNN algorithm can even be used in political science. You can take a potential voter and class them as either "will not vote" or "will vote" based on their characteristics and how they stack up against others who have or haven't voted in the past. It is even possible to look at the information you have about the person and about others in your database to make a prediction on which party they will vote for.

Before we move on to some of the other things that you can do with Python machine learning, we need to take a look at some of the benefit and some of the drawbacks of working with this kind of algorithm. To start are the benefits. You will find that there are many different benefits that come with using this kind of algorithm in your data science. Some of the best benefits will include:

1. When you use the KNN machine learning algorithm, there is not going to be an assumption about the data. What this means is

that this kind of algorithm is going to work well when you bring in nonlinear data to look over.

2. You will find that the KNN algorithm is going to be simple to use, while also helping you to explain how things work to others, especially when those others don't have any knowledge of machine learning.

3. The KNN algorithm s going to contain a lot of accuracy inside of it. There are a few models of supervised machine learning that you can work with, but for the level that comes with this one, you will find that it will work for your needs.

4. You can bring out the KNN algorithm to help out with a wide variety of problems that you need to handle. This is a good algorithm to use when you have a regression problem and with classification problems. You may need to change things up a bit, but you can make it work for both kinds of problems.

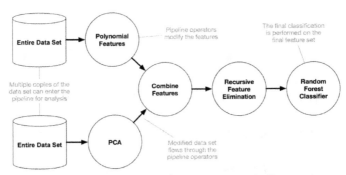

With those in mind, it is also important to take a look at some of the drawbacks that come with the KNN algorithm. It doesn't matter how great an algorithm appears, there are always going to be a few drawbacks that come with it, and the KNN algorithm is going to be no different. Some of the reasons why this algorithm may not be the best for all of the machine learning problems that you are trying to work with will include:

1. When it comes to computation, the KNN algorithm is going to get pretty expensive. The reason for this is that the KNN algorithm is going to function by storing all of your training data.

2. To make this kind of algorithm work, you have to make sure that your computer or system has a lot of memory to store all the information. Depending on the kind of system that you are working with, this can sometimes be hard to handle.

3. Any training data that you add to the algorithm is going to be stored. This is going to take up a lot of space on your computer. If you don't have enough space on the computer, then this algorithm is not going to work all that well.

4. When it comes to the stage for making predictions in this process, you may notice that the KNN algorithm is not going to be as fast as some of the other learning algorithms that you are able to pick.

5. If you add in any features that are irrelevant to the mixture, then the KNN algorithm is going to be really sensitive to this. It is also sensitive when you try to scale the data. This is going to make things hard if you have data that needs to be updated on a regular basis.

There are a lot of things to love about the KNN algorithm, but there are also times when it is not going to be the best option for you. Learning how this algorithm works, and when you are able to use it to get the best results possible. There are times when this is going to work well, and times when you need to avoid it, but it is definitely a machine learning algorithm that has a time and place, and it is one that you should take the time to learn more about.

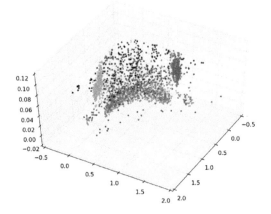

Chapter 4: Data Wrangling Visualization and Aggregation

We are now going to take some time to look at the idea of data wrangling. This is going to be the process where we are going to transform and then map data from one raw form into another format. The reason that we are going to want to do this is to make the data more appropriate and valuable for a lot of other purposes. Often the purpose is going to be to analyze the data that we have on hand.

There are going to be a lot of ways that you are able to do this. You may want to due to data visualization, data aggregation, spend the time training your own statistical model, and other options as well. Data wrangling is going to be a process that will follow a set of general steps, usually with the beginning of extracting data in its raw form from the source of the data. Then you can wrangle the raw data with a variety of algorithms, such as sorting, or you can prase the data into some predefined structures. And then this ends with depositing the content you get into some storage to use later on.

This kind of data transformation is going to be applied to some entities that are distinct, like in data values, columns, rows, and fields, within the same set of data. And some of the steps that you are going to use to make this happen could include parsing, joining, extractions, cleansing, consolidating, augmenting, and even filtering. The steps that you use are going to depend on what is needed in order to wrangle the outputs later on.

The recipients who get this information are often going to be a data scientist or data architect who will take the time to look through the data a bit further. These are often hired by business owners or users who will read through the reports made. They often want this spelled out for them so that they can use data they have to make informed decisions for the future of their own business.

Depending on how much data is coming in and how it needs to be formatted, this process was traditionally performed in a manual manner. It could be done through a spreadsheet for example. Or sometimes it is done with a hand-written script with the help of the R, SQL, or Python languages. Statistical data analysis and data mining are often used to make this a bit faster as well.

Now that we have a little look at how this works and what it means, it is time to take a closer look at some of the different things that you are able to do with your data, and how you are able to use all of this to get the best results out of any data you add into a machine learning algorithm.

Data Cleansing

The first thing that we are going to take a look at is the idea of data cleansing. This is going to be a process that a data scientist is able to go through in order to detect and either fix or deletes any records that are corrupt or inaccurate from their set of data. Inaccurate, incorrect, and even irrelevant parts of data can mess with the results that you get, so getting them under control and removing them or fixing them can make a big difference. Often this data cleansing is going to be performed interactively with some of the tools that are found with data wrangling.

After cleaning it up, the set of data should end up being pretty consistent with the other sets of data that you have in the system. The inconsistencies that are detected or which have been removed may have been caused by user errors, corruption in the storage that you used, or with different definitions in the data dictionary. Data cleaning is going to be a bit different from data validation though, so keep these separate.

For data cleansing to work, there need to be a few parts that come together to help us figure out how the data works and whether it is acting in the way that it should. Data that is considered high-quality needs to be able to pass a few criteria first. Some of these include

1. Validity: This is going to be the amount that the data is able to conform to the pre-defined rules or constraints of the business. Some examples of how this can work will include the following:

a. Data type constraints. This is when the values that fall in a column need to come from a certain type of data, such as a date or a numerical value.

b. Range constraints: This means that the dates or the numbers in the column need to fall inside a certain range. There will be a minimum or maximum value that is allowed.

c. Mandatory constraints. This one is going to focus on the idea that none of the columns are allowed to be empty in the set of data.

d. Unique constraints: This is where a field or even a combination of fields, needs to be unique across a set of data. You may put this in place to make sure that no two people on the form put in the same social security number.

e. Set membership constraints: This one would be telling the program that there needs to be an answer in there with a discrete value of codes. It could be something like gender in there.

 f. Regular expression patterns. There are times when a field is going to need to be validated with this way. You may choose to have a phone number match up in a certain way if you would like.

2. Accuracy: Accuracy is one that is hard to achieve with the help of data cleansing because it is going to require that everything can access a source of data that is external and that is going to contain the true value. Accuracy is able to be reached in some contexts of cleansing notably with customer contact data when it is able to use an external database to match up geographical locations and zip codes for example.

3. Completeness: The degree to which all required measures are known. Of course, this one is

really hard to work with when you are doing a data cleansing method.

4. Consistency: This is going to be the degree by which a set of measures are equivalent to across systems. It is possible that an inconsistency occurs when there are two items in your data set that happen to contractive each other.

5. Uniformity This is going to be the degree to which a set of data measures are specified using the same units of measure in all system. For example, if you pool together some data from different locations, it is possible that measurements may be in different terms.

There are a few issues that can come up when it is time to work with data cleansing. The first issue is with correcting errors and losing information in the process. This is one of the biggest issues, especially when you want to try and correct the values to remove entries that are not valid and any duplicates that come up. In many situations, the available information on these situations is going to be limited, and it is not going to have enough information to help you make the right corrections or changes.

What this ends up doing is that the primary solution to this issue is going to be to delete these entries. The deletion of data is not always a good thing though because it means that you are going to lose a lot of information, information that could be important to what you are trying to do, and it can skew the results and the predictions that you end up making.

The next issue that you need to take a look at here is maintaining the cleansed data. Cleaning your data can be expensive and it is going to take up a lot of time. so, after you have gone through and cleaned the data, and you have double checked that the data is free of errors, you want to try and avoid having to do it all of the time. You need to make sure that you only repeat this when you know the values have changed. Overall, this means that the lineage for cleansing has to be kept, which requires a lot of data collection and management techniques. Some companies and businesses just don't have the time or resources to do this.

Data cleansing framework can cause some issues. There are a lot of situations where it is not possible to derive a complete data-cleansing graph to help guide how the process should beave in advance. This is going to make it so that the cleansing process is going to be iterative, involving a lot of exploration and interaction. This is going to require a framework in the form of a collection of methods for error detection and elimination, along with a lot of auditing of your information. This requires a lot of time and energy to make it happen.

Data editing

The next thing that we need to take a look at when it comes to the data that we can use is the idea of data editing. This is going to be the process of involving a review, and then any adjustments that are necessary, of collected survey data. The purpose of doing this is to control the quality of the data that you decide to collect. You are able to edit the data in a manual manner, you can use Python to make this happen, or sometimes it helps to do a combination of both of these to see the best results.

There are actually a few different methods of editing that you are able to work with. The first one is going to be interactive editing. This type is going to be reserved for most of the modern methods that are manual but uses a computer to help. Most of the tools that are used will allow you to check the specified edits both during and after you enter it. And you can go through and correct any of the data that you need right away if you find it necessary. There are a few approaches that you are able to use here in order to correct some of the data that is wrong and these include:

1. Recontact the person who put in the information.
2. Compare the data from that user to the data they put in the previous year.
3. Compare the data of the user to the data that other similar respondents have put in at some point in the past.

4. Use the subject matter knowledge of the human editor to fill in the information based on their own knowledge along the way.

You will find that when it comes to editing, this interactive method is going to be the standard to use. It is used for both continuous and categorical data if you have them. Many editors like to use this because it has the ability to reduce the time frame that is needed to complete the cyclical process of adjusting after the review.

The next kind of editing that you are able to use is going to be selective editing. This is going to just be an umbrella term for a few methods you can use to identify any outliers and influential errors that come up. This technique is going to aim to work with interactive editing on a chosen subset of the records. This is going to help you to get more information when you are short on time and can help you get so much more out of the editing process.

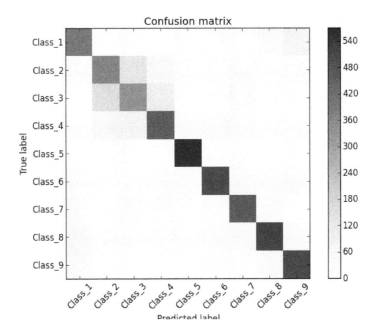

Now there are going to be two streams that you can work with here. There is the critical stream which is going to be any of the records that are going to be the most likely to contain some of those major errors. These are the ones that need to be edited using the more traditional interactive manner we talked about before. Then there is the non-critical stream. These may have errors, but it is less likely to have ones that are going to influence anything.

There are two methods of macro editing that you are able to work with. The aggregation method is going to be followed by most statistical agencies before publication. You are going to take some time to verify whether figures that are going to be published even seem possible. This is going to be done when you compare quantities in publication tables with the same quantities that showed up in earlier publications. If this is done and there seems to be an unusual value that is seen, a micro-editing procedure is going to be applied to the individual records, and the field that seems to contribute to the suspicious quantity.

Then there is the distribution method. This one is going to use the distribution of variables to help. Then it is going to compare all of the values that are there with the distribution. Records that happen to contain values that are seen as uncommon based on the distribution, then these are going to be checked out a bit more, and even edited too.

And finally, there is going to be a process that is known as automatic editing. This is going to record that will be done all on a computer, without any intervention by a human. There needs to be some prior knowledge on the values of a single variable or a combination of variables can be formulated as a set of edit rules which specify or constrain the admissible values.

Data scraping

In most cases, the transfer of data between one program to another is going to be done with data structures that are suited for automated processing. This is going to be done by a computer rather than by a person. This interchange in formats and protocols is going to be structured in a rigid manner, which makes it easier for us to know that it is going to work out well.

This means that the key element that will make data scraping a bit different from regular parsing is that the output that is being scraped is going to be intended for display to an end user, rather than as an input to be used by another program. This means that this information is not going to be documented, and it is not going to be structured for convenient parsing.

When we take a look at data scraping, we are going to have to ignore binary data, display formatting, superfluous commentary, redundant labels, and any other information that is seen as irrelevant. And in some cases, the information is going to be taken out if it is seen as hindering the process of automation.

Data scraping is a process that is going to be done either to interface a legacy system or to interface a third-party system that is not going to have an API that is convenient. In the latter scenario, the operator of the system is going to be able to see screen scraping as unwanted, mostly because it is going to cause a big increase in the load of the system. It also will cut out the revenue that can be gained from advertising, and there is a lot of loss in the amount of control that you have over the content that comes in.

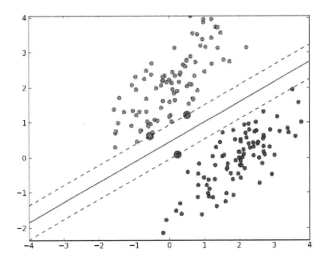

Data scraping is something that is seen as an ad-hoc inelegant technique. What this means is that it is seen as the last resort, usually only brought out when no other mechanism to interchange the data is usable. Aside from the overhead for processing and programming that is so high, the output displays intended for humans to look at are going to change often. Humans are able to cope with this and figure it out, but the program may end up reporting what looks like nonsense, and it won't be able to check the validity of what it sees.

There are a few technical variants that you are able to use here. The first one is going to be screen scraping. This is a technique that will capture old screens and then try to take the data and change it over to something that is a bit more modern. Some of the more modern forms of screen scraping that you are going to see will include the program capturing the bit map data that is found on the screen and then it will put it through an OCR engine. With the help of GUI applications and a query of the graphical controls, we are going to end up with a sequence of screens that can be captured on an automatic basis and then converted into a database that you are able to work with.

Then we can move on to web scraping. When we look at a web page, we will notice that they will have a coding language that is based on text, such as HTML, and this means that they come with a lot of data that you can use in text form. However, since humans are the ones who go through these web pages and use them, these pages are not created for automated use. This is why there are a few tool kits that were designed to help with scraping web content as well.

There are several companies who have come up with systems for web scraping that are going to try and copy the human processing that occurs when they view a webpage. The hope here is that these systems will be able to automatically extract the information that is useful out of the page, making it easier for others to use.

In addition, there are large websites that are going to use some defensive algorithms in the hopes of protecting their data from web scrapers. They do this by placing a limit on how many requests an IP or an IP network is able to send out. This is going to be an ongoing battle. Website developers want to be able to scrape the information in order to find the most valuable content, but they don't want hackers and more to be able to get onto the website and cause issues as well.

And finally, there is the idea of report mining. This is when there is an extraction of the data from human-readable computer reports. With data extraction that is conventional, it needs a connection to a working source system, a suitable connectivity standard or API, and some complex querying to make it happen. By using the standard reporting options for that system, and making sure that the output is directed out to a spool file rather than a printer, it is possible for the static reports to be generated in the right way.

The reason that this method is used is that it is helpful in avoiding a lot of usage of the CPU during regular business hours, can help with quick reports, even customized ones, and can minimize the license costs for ERP customers. While web scraping and data scraping are going to involve having to interact with a dynamic report, this kind of mining is going to be the process of extracting out data from files that come in formats that people can read. You will be able to generate this information and these reports through almost any system that you find, and all you need to do is intercept the data feed over to the printer.

As you can see, there are a lot of different things that you are able to do with your system when it comes to using the data and visualizing it. Working with some of the techniques that we talked about in this chapter, along with a few others, you will be able to really see the difference in how well your system is going to work and what kind of data you are able to pull up and use for your needs.

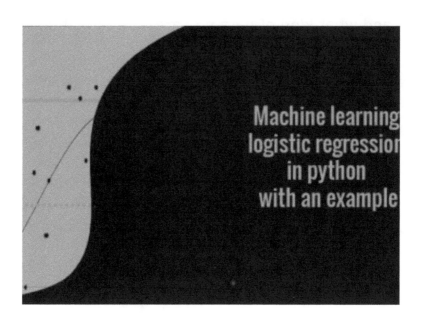

Chapter 5 Django and Web Application

As we discussed a bit earlier on in this guidebook, machine learning is slowly making its way to a lot of different sectors when it comes to all the fields and businesses that are able to use it. In fact, pretty much all business segments have started to use machine learning at some point or another. Machine learning has been able to take a role in our daily lives, and it is slowly but surely starting to represent something that is pretty well-known and concrete in the minds of the public.

However, just because it is more recent and is just starting to grow, don't be fooled into thinking that it is going to be a cutting edge option or it is only for businesses that have a ton of money to keep up with the latest and greatest in the technology. In fact, machine learning and some of the techniques that come with it have been around for some time, and you will find that ignoring machine learning can be a bad thing for your business.

Think of it this way, do you see it as a waste of the time of your employees to work on a task that could be automated and done for them? Is it a waste of your valuable data when it just sits in a database, waiting for someone to have the time and resources to get to it? Or do you feel that it is a waste of the final product when it is delivered without being able to reach the full capacity of what it should be able to do? If you answered yes to any, but most likely all, of these questions, then machine learning is something that you need to spend some time on.

But here comes the next question, how are you able to implement machine learning in business, implanting it as a tool for your engineers or as a service for your clients? How do you streamline it without having to have experts in the field handle it all of the time? That is what we are going to explore in this chapter!

Working with an API in machine learning

One of the practical methods that you are able to do all of the things we discussed above for machine learning is to bring out an API. Offering a machine learning solution with the help of this API is going to allow a person to focus more on the results, while still ensuring that the developers you have working on machine learning have full control to maintain the model that comes with it.

Using the API is going to prove itself as an efficient way of delivering machine learning. This is true even with companies who have large AI divisions and who will really apply this in an extensive manner, such as what we see with Google and Amazon.

Now we need to go back to the idea of some of the advances that come with Machine learning. Another factor that we need to consider for its role in why this method is being adopted so well is because of the exceptional libraries that come with Python. Python is one of the best languages to use with machine learning because of all that you are able to do with it, and you will find the libraries are going to be even better. In particular, you will find that some of the libraries like TensorFlow, pandas, and scikit-learn are going to make it so much easier for your developers to come up with solutions that are high quality in machine learning.

You can easily see why the Python language is going to be the most used programming language in data science and machine learning. Nothing else even comes close! The language is not only simple enough for a beginner to use and learn, but it is also going to have the power and functionality to handle some of the more complex tasks that you are going to do in machine learning.

One thing that we need to take a look at here is the idea of Django from Python. This is going to be a web framework that is open sourced and available with Python (it has been fully written in Python so you know you are going to be able to handle it with some of the things we have discussed in this guidebook). Django is really easy to get started with, it has the stability that you need, and it is already integrated with the libraries that come with Python, so you won't have to worry about that.

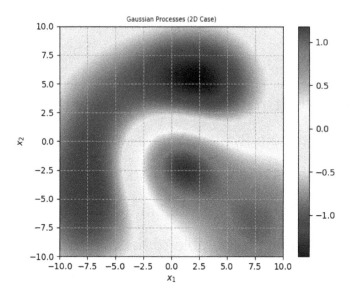

The Django web framework was first developed because there were several developers of a newspaper's online site who were tired of the type of framework that they were using at the time. They wanted to be able to work with a Python version and use it to build up the backend that was needed of the portal. Because of this need, Django was developed.

Since it was first developed, Django has seen a lot of success, mainly form its ease of use. You will find that over time, it has grown to become one of the top four web frameworks that are being used on many businesses and websites. In fact, some major websites like Disqus and Instagram are already using this framework to keep themselves up and running.

Plus, this framework is going to be able to help you out with a lot of the major issues and questions that you run into when it is time to implement machine learning and the Python language online. Adding to the Django REST Framework and a web server of your choices (working with Guincorn is a great option if you are looking for one), it is possible for you to get a Python-based API up and running in no time, allowing you to work with the solution that you need with machine learning.

More about Django

Let's take a closer look at some of the things you should know about Django and how to use it. Django is a framework that was written out in Python. A framework is just going to be a collection of modules that are brought together in a manner that makes development easier on those who are using it. These are going to be put in a program together and this allows you to create a website or another application using an existing source, rather than having to start straight from nothing each time.

This is how many websites, even those that are developed at home by one person, are able to include some more advanced features and functionality, including contact forms, file upload support, management, and admin panels, comment boxes and more. Whether you want to create a web application for yourself or for a business, you will find that using a framework like Django could give you a high-quality product without having to be a programmer on your own. By using the Django framework, the components that you need for this are going to be in there already, you just have to take the time to configure them in the proper manner to match your site.

When we take a look at the official site for Django, it is basically a high-level web framework from Python that is going to encourage the rapid development of a project, along with a design that is pragmatic and clean. This framework, even though it is open sourced, was built up by developers experienced in Python, and it takes care of a lot of the hassle that comes with web development. This allows a lot of people to work on this framework, even if they have no web development experience to go from.

When we use a framework like Django or some of the other ones, it makes life easier. The framework is going to take care of the web development part so that you are able to focus on writing your app, without having to reinvent the wheel and start from the beginning each time. plus, Django is open sourced and free, making it the perfect choice for those who want to create their own website and those who need to do it for a company or business.

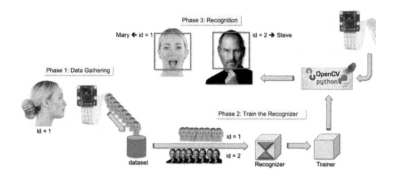

Django is going to be a great option to use because it offers us a big collection of modules that you are able to use with any of the web-based projects you want to focus with. Mainly though, the Django framework was designed in order to save wasted time for developers and to make life easier.

Another thing that you may find interesting when it comes to Django is that it was created with the idea that front end developers would be the ones most likely to use it. The template language is going to be designed in a way to make you feel comfortable, and it is going to be easy for anyone to learn in order to work with HTML, including front end developers and designers. But it is also going to be easily extensible and flexible, allowing developers to augment the template language as needed.

If you do plan to do some work with machine learning and Python, especially if you are trying to do this with web design and web applications, it is a good idea to bring in the Django framework to help you out. There are a lot of different ways that you can use, and it is going to make your life easier.

How to get started with Django

Now that we understand a bit more about Django and what it is all about, it is time to move on to a few of the other things that you are able to do with this program. Django is going to adhere to what is known as the MVT architectural pattern, or model view template. After you have taken the time to install it and you have all of the necessary information and files in place for it, you will need to get to executing it. The command that is needed to do this includes:

Django-admin startproject mysite

When you work with this command, it is going to create most of the configurations and structure that you need for that folder to get the project up and running. Once you have given that command some time to get up and running, it is time to get yourself into the folder for the project. Any time that you want to do this, work with the following code:

Python manage.py startapp myapp

At this point, you have created the app that is going to be able to run the correct machine learning API that you need. Next, you need to take some time to edit out the models/py of the app, that is, if you plan to use a database to go along with this project. And don't forget to take some time to create what is known as the API Views to make this all work together well.

For the most part, you will find that your machine learning model is going to be accessed from this API Views when you need it. This means you just need to add the views.py file to the mix to get it. One of the methods that you can use to make the integration of the model and the server happen is that, when you are done building and then validating the model to make sure it works, you will save up any of the binaries that come up with Pickle. From there, you can add all of these codes into a package, and then import them over to the View.

In addition to this, there are times when you may find the model is going to be too large for the storage you have, or it may be too large for other reasons. If this is true of your file, then it is a good idea to load this in a new way, as a global variable in this file. This ensures that the file is only going to load one time. Traditionally, this is going to load up every time that you try to call up the view. When the file is large, this is going to slow down the computer and can even cause things to get stuck. But with the steps that we just did, we are basically asking it to just load up once, any time that you start up the server, rather than each time you start up the View.

As you can see here, there are a lot of great features that you are able to use when it comes to Django. It is a fast and reliable way for you to take some of your machine learning models and get them to work for you. And it works in Python which can make things even easier for you to work with. Taking the time to get it downloaded and making sure you get it set up with the right Python libraries will ensure that it is ready to handle any of the web-based models that you would like to do with your project.

Grid Layout

Important parameter

Random Layout

Important parameter

Chapter 6: A Look at the Neural Networks

The final thing that we are going to take a look at in this guidebook is the idea of neural networks and how they will work with Python, and with machine learning. Neural networks are going to be one of the frameworks that you can do in machine learning, one that tries to mimic the way that the natural biological neural networks in humans are going to operate.

The human mind is pretty amazing. It is able to look at a lot of different things around us and identify patterns with a very high degree of accuracy. Any time that you go on a drive and see a cow, for example, you will recognize it at a cow. This applies to any animal or other things that you are going to see when you are out on the road. The reason that we are able to do this is that we have learned over a period of time how these items look, and what can differentiate one item from another.

The goal of an artificial neural network is to be able to mimic, as much as possible, the way that the human brain is able to work. It is a complex architecture to make this happen. But when it is in place, it allows the system to do a lot of amazing things that it would not be able to do in other situations. Let's take a look at how these neural networks can work, and why they are so amazing for our work with machine learning.

A neuron is going to be made up of the body of a cell, with a few extensions that come from it. The majority of these extensions are going to be in the form of a branch that is known as a dendrite. A long process, or a branching, is going to exist and this part is known as the axon. The transmission of signals begin at a region in this axon, and that is going to be known as the hillock.

The neuron is going to have a boundary that we like to call the cell membrane. A potential difference is going to exist between the outside and the inside of this cell membrane, and that difference is called the membrane. If you are able to get the input to be big enough, then some action potential is going to be generated. This action potential will then travel all the way down the axon and head away from the body of the cell.

A neuron is going to come next. This neuron is connected up with another neuron, and on down the line, with the help of a synapse. The information is going to head out of the neuron through the axon and then it is passed on to the synapses and to the neuron which is going to receive the message. Note that the neuron is only going to fire once the threshold has gone above the amount that is specified. The signals in this process are going to be important because they are going to be received by the other neurons in the chain. The neurons are going to use signals to help them communicate with one another.

When it comes to the synapses, they can either be excitatory or inhibitory. When a spike or a signal arrives in one of the excitatory synapses, the receiving neuron is going to be caught on fire. If the signals are going to be inhibitory, then the neuron is not going to be fired onward.

The synapses and the cell body are going to be able to work together to calculate the differences that are there between the excitatory inputs and the inhibitory inputs. If there is a big difference here, then the neurons are told to fire the message on down the line.

These types of networks are going to be used a lot because they are great at learning and analyzing patterns by looking at it in several different layers. Each layer that it goes through will spend its time seeing if there is a pattern that is inside the image. If the neural network does find a new pattern, it is going to activate the process to help the next layer start. This process will continue going on and on until all the layers in that algorithm are created and the program is able to predict what is in the image.

Now, there are going to be several things that are going to happen from this point. If the algorithm went through all the layers and then was able to use that information to make an accurate prediction, the neurons are going to become stronger. This results in a good association between the patterns and the object and the system will be more efficient at doing this the next time you use the program.

This may seem a bit complicated so let's take a look at how these neural networks will work together. Let's say that you are trying to create a program that can take the input of a picture and then recognize that there is a car in that picture. It will be able to do this based on the features that are in the car, including the color of the car, the number on the license plate, and even more.

When you are working with some of the conventional coding methods that are available, this process can be really difficult to do. You will find that the neural network system can make this a really easy system to work with.

For the algorithm to work, you would need to provide the system with an image of the car. The neural network would then be able to look over the picture. It would start with the first layer, which would be the outside edges of the car. Then it would go through a number of other layers that help the neural network understand if there were any unique characteristics that are present in the picture that outlines that it is a car. If the program is good at doing the job, it is going to get better at finding some of the smallest details of the car, including things like its windows and even wheel patterns.

Now, when you are working on this, you may notice that there could potentially be a ton of layers that work with it. The more details and the more layers that you decide to find, the more accurate the prediction with the neural network is going to be. When there are more layers, there are more chances that the algorithm is going to be able to learn along the way. From then on, the algorithm is going to get better at making predictions and will be able to do it with more accuracy, and faster, from now one.

This is a good algorithm to use when you want to have it recognize pictures, or even with some of the facial recognition software that is out there. With these, there is no possible way that you can input all of the possible information that is needed. So working with the neural networks, where the program is able to learn things along the way, can really make a difference in whether the program is going to work or not.

Backpropagation

For you to work on training a neural network to do a certain task at the right time, the units of each part need to be adjusted. This ensures that there is a reduction in the amount of error that happens between the target output and the actual output. What this means is that the derivatives of the weights need to be computed by the network. So, this means that the network has to be able to monitor the changes in error as the weights are decreased or increased based on the situation. The backpropagation algorithm is the one that you will choose to use to help you figure this part out.

If you plan on having the network units you work with becoming linear, then this is an easy enough algorithm to understand. With the linear options, the algorithm is going to be able to get the error derivative of the weights by determining the rate at which the error is changing as the unit's activity level is being changed.

When we are looking at the situation with the output units, the derivative of the error is going to be obtained when we can figure out the difference between the target output and the real output. To help us find any change rate in error for the hidden unit in a layer, all the weights between the hidden unit and the output unit which it has been connected to has to be determined ahead of time.

To help us with this part, we then need to go through and multiply the weights by error derivatives in the weights and then the product that is added together. The answer that you are able to get here is going to be equal to the change rate in error for your hidden unit.

Once you have this error change rate, you can then go through and calculate the error change rate for all of the other layers that you want to work with. The calculation that you get for these is going to be done from one layer to the next and in the opposite direction from where you would like the message to head through the network.

Outlier detection

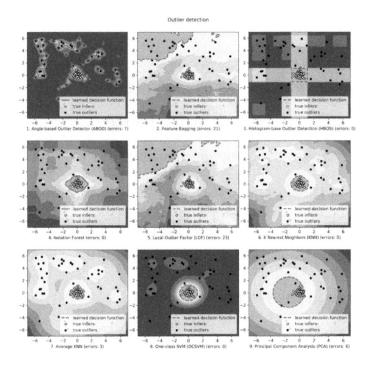

Conclusion

Thank for making it through to the end of *Python Machine Learning*, let's hope it was informative and able to provide you with all of the tools you need to achieve your goals whatever they may be.

The next step is to get started with some of the coding and more that we have spent time talking about in this guidebook. There are so many great things that you are able to do when it comes to Python machine learning, and this industry and field is just starting to be explored. Being able to look through some of the different topics that we brought up, and learning how to do some of the work, can make a difference at how well you will be able to utilize this field for your own.

This guidebook took some time to look at a lot of the different aspects of machine learning that you are able to do with the help of the Python language. Whether you want to work with supervised learning, unsupervised learning, or even reinforcement learning, you will find that this guidebook has the options that will work for you. We will break apart a lot of different problems and then use the Python coding language to help us get the work done the right way.

When you are ready to learn more about Python machine learning and how it is going to work well for you, make sure to check out this guidebook and get started today!

Finally, if you found this book useful in any way, a review on Amazon is always appreciated!

CPSIA information can be obtained
at www.ICGtesting.com
Printed in the USA
LVHW050758120221
679113LV00016B/526